Easter Me, O God!

❧

Reflections
For the Resurrection Season

Year B

Rev. Trish Sullivan Vanni, PhD

ISBN: 978-1-7369057-0-8

DEDICATION

With gratitude for the life and leadership of
Fr. Tim Power, who gave so freely and so abundantly.
He was an Easter person, and I was blessed to have
him as my friend and mentor.

✦

Offered with love to the
Charis Ecumenical Catholic Community.
Your energy and enthusiasm for the Gospel
empower my dreams and light up my life.
And with gratitude to my husband Pete and our
children, Nora plus Hank, Justin, and Mairead.
I am who I am thanks to all of you

NOTE FROM THE AUTHOR

The scripture quotations in this book are taken from the World English Bible Catholic Edition (WEBC), which is in the public domain.

Out of respect for the Jewish community, the tetragrammaton YHWH is not made into a pronounceable English word. Instead, the word Adonai is used per the suggestion of rabbi friends. Similarly, the word Judeans is substituted for Jews, a word that was coined in the 12th century. This translation was fuel for centuries of antisemitism, particularly driven by the strident language of the Gospel of John, which is featured in this cycle of readings.

The scripture readings are drawn from the daily lectionary. The supplementary readings are things that spoke to me. The prayers I offer are questions I am prayers that I propose for myself. I hope that by sharing them, they might be useful on your journey, as well.

Trish

1.

EASTER

Very early on the first day of the week, they came to the tomb
when the sun had risen. They were saying among themselves,
"Who will roll away the stone from the door of the tomb for
us?" for it was very big. Looking up, they saw that the stone
was rolled back. *– Mark 16:1-4*

☙

The Day of Resurrection! O People, let us be radiant. It is
Pascha, the Lord's Passover; for Christ God has carried us
over from death to life, from earth to heaven, as we sing a
victory hymn. *– St. John of Damascus*

———————◆———————

At some point in elementary school, most American
children read E.B. White's beautiful novel *Charlotte's Web*.
In it, they encounter a remarkable tale of love and
solidarity, loss and triumph in the form of an unlikely
friendship between a young girl, Fern, the runt pig she
raises, Wilbur, and an unforgettably wise spider,
Charlotte. It is a story of death but also of salvation.

Charlotte saves Wilbur from the journey to pork chops
by writing words into her web in his pen. With each
word, Wilbur's self-concept expands. He goes from
being "Some Pig" to "Radiant." Truly. He bats his eyes,
does a backflip. No longer can anyone imagine him
becoming bacon.

I don't remember many times that I have felt radiant,
but shame on me! Because that is what the resurrection
looks like: inbreaking light illuminating all, shining out on
the world through all. We are participants in this Easter
transformation. "Some Disciples. Radiant!"

**Radiant, resurrection God, shine in and through me this
Easter Season until my radiance reflects yours!**

2.

1ST MONDAY

They departed quickly from the tomb with fear and great joy,
and ran to bring his disciples word. As they went to tell his
disciples, behold, Jesus met them, saying, "Rejoice!"
– Matthew 28:8-10

❧

I love the ocean, I fear the ocean... But I've realized the shore
only feels safe because it seems more predictable—and of
course it isn't. Life is always uncontrollable. Fear is a natural
reaction to that. Joy, love, and passion—these are what we
feel when we take the plunge anyways, knowing we're brave
enough to accept the risk. *– Lori Duschene*

In my experience, life doesn't seem to come at us in
single emotions. Invariably, it's a blend. I'm ecstatic that
I'm pregnant; I'm scared of what childbirth may bring.
I'm excited that my youngster is brave enough to venture
north to language immersion camp; I'm worried she'll be
lonely and isolated if she can't speak English.

Fear and joy seem to be the sides of a single coin. No
surprise then, that the women who have discovered
Jesus lives are not only ecstatic but scared. What could
this miraculous occurrence mean? There's something to
celebrate but what will the future hold? They bear
amazing news but will anyone believe it?

In steps Jesus with the perfect antidote for the
moment: Drop the fear, stay in the joy! "Rejoice!" After
all, he is there. As he always is with us. "Bidden or not
bidden, God is present," said Carl Jung.

**When I stand in the crossroads of fear and joy, help me
choose joy, unbidden, unbounded God!**

3.

1ST TUESDAY

But Mary was standing outside at the tomb weeping. So as she wept, she stooped and looked into the tomb, and she saw two angels in white sitting, one at the head and one at the feet, where the body of Jesus had lain. They asked her, "Woman, why are you weeping?" She said to them, "Because they have taken away my Lord, and I don't know where they have laid him." – *John 20: 11-14*

❧

"And when your sorrow is comforted (time soothes all sorrows) you will be content that you have known me. You will always be my friend. You will want to laugh with me…

And your friends will be properly astonished to see you laughing as you look up at the sky!" – *Antoine de Saint-Exupéry*

We live in a culture that isolates and even denies space for grief. Too often, people are expected to rebound immediately when, in fact, the grieving process takes time. Integration of loss can be a lifetime journey.

The Little Prince was among the books I most cherished as an adolescent. I look back now and realize that it may be because it helped me navigate a very deep personal loss. The Prince leaves but he affirms that he will remain. Those he loves who simply have to look at the sky to see him – and they will laugh.

We have a great blessing in Mary of Magdala. She has loved her teacher deeply and is grieving fully. In her, we find permission to be authentic in times of loss. She is first to the tomb and also first to express the depth of grief. No surprise that in her honesty she is also the first to experience the power of the resurrection.

St. Mary of Magdala, intercede from me when the weight of my grief prevents me from gazing toward the sky.

4.

1ST WEDNESDAY

"When he had sat down at the table with them, he took the bread and gave thanks. Breaking it, he gave it to them. Their eyes were opened and they recognized him; then he vanished out of their sight. They said to one another, "Weren't our hearts burning within us while he spoke to us along the way, and while he opened the Scriptures to us?" – *Luke 24: 30-32*

❧

Unfathomable darkness and emptiness—the great nada of John of the Cross—can be transformed, not by any human effort or artificial lights, but by simply persevering with unquenchable yearning in the heart of darkness. Then the terrible abyss metamorphoses into a bridal chamber, because we have given God the space to show the full extent of his relentlessly faithful love. – *Erasmo Leiva-Merikakis*

───────────◆───────────

I've always had a deep fondness for the couple – very likely Cleopas and his spouse – who are dragging themselves back home to Emmaus, crushed in the aftermath of the crucifixion. It's the rare human being who goes the distance of a full life without spending some time thrust into despair. Our human losses – of people and places(not to mention all the other things that feel like big or small deaths) can leave us enervated and even hopeless.

Like the Emmaus couple, our road can feel long and bereft. How beautiful that they are surprised by healing, which comes to them, at first, anonymously. How powerful to meet the healing stranger, and then discover the presence of the living Christ.

In this Easter season, help me see you O Christ, particularly in unexpected faces and places.

5.

1ˢᵗ THURSDAY

Then he opened their minds, that they might understand the Scriptures. He said to them, "Thus it is written, and thus it was necessary for the Christ to suffer and to rise from the dead the third day, and that repentance and remission of sins should be preached in his name to all the nations, beginning at Jerusalem. You are witnesses... – *Luke 24: 45-48*

❧

The Emmaus story reveals to us the image of a God and a church that walk alongside human confusion, human pain and human loss of faith and hope. Emmaus challenges us to see that it isn't our unshakeable faith and deep spirituality that connect us with the risen Christ, but our smallest gestures of hospitality and friendship. – *Amy Hunter*

I don't know about you, but sometimes I wonder if I overcomplicate discipleship. Too often, I compare myself to impossible exemplars like Mother Teresa or Martin Luther King Jr. Which is a set up. With that as a benchmark, I'll never measure up. And in an odd way, it strikes me that those comparisons in some way sort of take me off the hook.

I love the idea expressed by Amy Hunter. Perhaps living our connection to Christ, expressing our discipleship, doesn't require faith that moves mountains. Perhaps it's simply about extending loving kindness to others. My grandmothers were women of amazing faith. No one ever walked into their home without being welcomed with warmth and hospitality. Their love of neighbor was a close match to their love of God.

God, help me remember that living your path is also found in the latte dates of life and doors that are opened with a smile.

6.

1ST FRIDAY

He said to them, "Cast the net on the right side of the boat,
and you will find some." They cast it therefore, and now they
weren't able to draw it in for the multitude of fish. That
disciple therefore whom Jesus loved said to Peter, "It's the
Lord!" So when Simon Peter heard that it was the Lord, he
wrapped his coat around himself (for he was naked), and
threw himself into the sea. – *John 21: 6-7*

❧

Fishing provides that connection with the whole living world.
It gives you the opportunity of being totally immersed,
turning back into yourself in a good way. A form of
meditation, some form of communion with levels of yourself
that are deeper than the ordinary self. – *Ted Hughes*

Now that I've spent a few decades in Minnesota, it
makes more sense to me that Jesus' first invites to join
him were extended to a bunch of fishermen. Fisherman
have a few precious, unique qualities.

First and foremost, they're persistent and patient. I'm
so not that way; I usually last about a half an hour
casting. Second, they are optimists. No fish today? Dang
it, Scarlett, tomorrow is another day! Set the alarm clock!

Of course the most out there, irrepressible of these
anglers is Peter. In a nanosecond of recognition, he's out
of the boat and into the sea, swimming to get to Jesus. I
love the guy. There is no moment but this, no action to
take but leaping forward.

**Help me see you, resurrection Lord, and when I do,
energize me to leap fully into your presence.**

7.

1ST SATURDAY

Now when he had risen early on the first day of the week, he appeared first to Mary Magdalene... She went and told those who had been with him as they mourned and wept. When they heard that he was alive and had been seen by her, they disbelieved. – *Mark 16:9-11*

❧

Bad news travels at the speed of light; good news travels like molasses. – *Tracy Morgan*

"There's good news, and there's bad news..." We've all heard these jokes. Like the Catholic who got a phone call from Jesus, who said "I have good news and bad news." The person said, "Tell me the good news!" "The good news is that I'm back." "And the bad news?" "I'm calling from Salt Lake City."

What's up with the guys? They are devastated, mourning and weeping. But when the first witness to the resurrection comes to tell them that Jesus lives, they hold fast to their grief. They refuse to believe.

Perhaps there are some things we resist because to trust that they are true sets us up, potentially, for even more devastation and disappointment if we're wrong. What if this Easter, we seized the promise of the resurrection and all it implies with what one writer called the "fervor with which the drowning seize life preservers?" What if at the crossroads of belief and disbelief, we choose belief?

When reluctance, resignation or cynicism seizes me, help me see that you are right there Lord – and not just calling in from Salt Lake City.

8.

2ND SUNDAY

Mary Magdalene came and told the disciples that she had seen the Lord, and that he had said these things to her. When therefore it was evening on that day, the first day of the week, and when the doors were locked where the disciples were assembled, for fear of the Jews, Jesus came and stood in the middle and said to them, "Peace be to you." – *John 20: 18-19*

❧

Never be in a hurry; do everything quietly and in a calm spirit. Do not lose your inner peace for anything whatsoever, even if your whole world seems upset. – *Saint Francis de Sales*

You know there's turmoil afoot when the very first words someone speaks to a gathered group is "Peace be to you." I can imagine what the time in the upper room was like before the arrival of Jesus. Who else would be killed? Dare they venture out? Should they continue to hide or flee to the outer regions to their familial homes and prior professions? It's interesting to me that Jesus speaks not from the entrance to the room, but from the middle of the gathered community. His presence, his peace, radiates from the center.

Building a peaceful center is what inspires me to maintain my commitment to meditation. In the silence, I am reminded of the God of love that dwells in the Center of my Being. I am reminded that I am connected to every human person, and all times and places. In that awareness, am much more receptive to the risen Christ's invitation, "Peace be to you."

Help me remember to place you in the center of my life, God of Peace, and seek you through prayer and meditation.

9.

2ND MONDAY

Jesus answered, "Most certainly I tell you, unless one is born
of water and Spirit, they can't enter into God's Kingdom.
That which is born of the flesh is flesh. That which is born of
the Spirit is spirit." – *John 3:5-6*

∽

I am a person who thinks about the nature of the Spirit when
I write. I think about what can't be known and only imagined.
I often sense a spirit or force or meaning beyond myself. I
leave it open as to what the Spirit is,
but I continue to make guesses. – *Amy Tan*

Once, on a retreat, we were asked to which of the three
persons of the Trinity we prayed. I had never thought
about that before. While we believe that the triune God
is one God, we also believe in this mysterious reality of
Father, Son and Holy Spirit.

Maybe Yoda is to blame, but for me, the Spirit has
always been in the foreground. There is a force moving
in all things, I believe. As a Christian, I name it "grace,"
and all grace is, when you simplify the theological
gymnastics, is the presence of God.

The Spirit became even more front and center for me
when I was introduced to the feminine translations
associated with it in the Hebrew Scriptures. *Shekhinah*,
the indwelling of God. *Ruach*, the breath of God.
Embracing the Spirit, it seems that not only does God
dwell in us but we, in fact, dwell in the midst of God.

Today, Spirit of God, let me rest in you.

10.

2ND TUESDAY

"The wind blows where it wants to, and you hear its sound, but don't know where it comes from and where it is going. So is everyone who is born of the Spirit." – *John 3: 8*

❧

Believe. No pessimist ever discovered the secrets of the stars, or sailed to an uncharted island, or opened a new heaven to the human spirit. – *Helen Keller*

The Gospels remind us that seeing is not a requirement for believing. There are many things that are unseen to me in which I nevertheless have faith. There's a Wi-Fi signal everywhere I go, and I can't tell you how that works to save my life. But I trust that it's there when I see bars on my phone or boot up my laptop and see the little radar symbol fully filled out.

I believe that faith does require trusting in what is unseen. Trusting that the glimmers of the divine that break in on us – the love of friends and family, the slow movement of humankind toward compassion and justice – hint at something more than what is visible to me. As does the glory of a sunset over the prairie or the drama of the clouds in a gathering Spring storm.

My spouse considers me an irredeemable optimist. I never plan enough time for travel. I return openhearted to relationships that have been bruised. Maybe that's the same part in my that says, "I believe." Of this, I don't repent!

Today, in moments of questioning, I pray the prayer of Thomas: "Lord, I believe. Help my unbelief."

11.

2ND WEDNESDAY

"For God so loved the world, that he gave his only born Son, that whoever believes in him should not perish, but have eternal life. For God didn't send his Son into the world to judge the world, but that the world should be saved through him.." – *John 3:16-17*

∽

Love is the whole thing. We are only pieces.
— *Jalaluddin Rumi*

"All you need is love. (Wah, wah, wah, wah, wah…)" sang The Beatles. I'm considering the possibility that this lyric might just be a profound theological statement. We fret and analyze what discipleship should look like (well, at least we pastor people do, since we are invited to invite others into it). But what if all that a Christian needs to empower a life of following Jesus is, in fact, love? He tells us that God is love, and those who abide in love abide in God and God in them. Love is the door.

That makes me believe that Rumi's beautiful observation can serve our self-concept as followers of Jesus and bearers of His Good News. After all, we are the embracers of a God that is love and a Son that is all about love and a Spirit that moves through the world in love. As John Lennon noted, all you need, it appears, is love. "Love is the whole thing."

God of love, help me remember that "love is the whole thing," and help me remember and radiate that I am in fact a piece of that stunning reality.

12.

2ᴺᴰ THURSDAY

"For he whom God has sent speaks the words of God; for God gives the Spirit without measure. The Father loves the Son, and has given all things into his hand." — *John 3: 34-35*

⁓

If nature has made you for a giver, your hands are born open, and so is your heart; and though there may be times when your hands are empty, your heart is always full, and you can give things out of that—warm things, kind things, sweet things—help and comfort and laughter.
— *Frances Hodgson Burnett*

If God is love, one of the other things it seems God "is" is giving. A beloved Benedictine professor of mine, Fr. Kevin, used to say (exhortatively no less), "God lives for giving!" I've always liked that image, as if God is poised over me waiting for my heart and hands to open.

The Easter Gospels underscore the magnitude of God's giving. Today John reminds us that the Spirit comes to us "without measure" from the Father. Unlimited God. And that the Son has been given all things by Creator God. Complete union.

I loved the novel *The Little Princess*, which is quoted above. Perhaps its my optimism, again, but I like to think that the quote should say not, "if" nature has made you a giver, but "because" it is our nature to be givers. We, like God, are made to pour out the good things – warmth, love, kindness, assurance. The task is to move closer to Fr. Kevin's image of God. To live for giving.

God of giving, open me to all you pour out, and help me channel you in all that I, in turn, give to others.

13.

2ND FRIDAY

Jesus took the loaves, and having given thanks, he distributed
to the disciples, and the disciples to those who were sitting
down, likewise also of the fish as much as they desired. When
they were filled, he said to his disciples, "Gather up the
broken pieces which are left over, that nothing be lost."
— *John 6:11-12*

❧

Leftovers make you feel good twice. First, when you put it
away, you feel thrifty and intelligent: "I'm saving food!" Then
a month later when blue hair is growing out of the ham, and
you throw it away, you feel really intelligent:
"I'm saving my life!" — *George Carlin*

———————————

Of the accounts of the feeding of the multitude, only in
John's Gospel does Jesus seem to be interested in the
leftovers. It's not enough that thousands have been fed
despite the initial scarcity of food. Get out the plastic
containers and get those pieces packaged up.

My spouse loves leftovers. I'm not going to regale you
with how tolerant he is of items that have marinated in
the frig for days on end. Let's just say that he is a man
who is not interested in waste. And even though I resist
reheated burritos and microwaved burgers, I've grown in
my ability to be grateful for that food when we "graze."

Jesus reminds us not only of God's abundance but of
the value of that abundance. That we can not only
cherish what we're given but make sure we are not
wasteful. Everything matters in God's world. Even the
smallest morsels, the crumbs, matter.

**When something seems insignificant or disposable, God,
help me see the value you have given everything.**

13

14.

2ND SATURDAY

When therefore they had rowed about twenty-five or thirty
stadia, they saw Jesus walking on the sea and drawing near to
the boat; and they were afraid. But he said to them,
"It is I. Don't be afraid." — *John 6:19-20*

❧

I learned that courage was not the absence of fear, but the
triumph over it. The brave man is not he who does not feel
afraid, but he who conquers that fear. — *Nelson Mandela*

More than once, people have said to me "fear is the
absence of faith." I know that saying has biblical roots,
but I'm not so sure I agree. I've dealt with a lot of
anxiety over the years, and that gripping, often paralyzing
emotion has sometimes knocked me off my pins. But
even at times of great fear, I have been able to access my
deep sense that God will stay with me, no matter what
the circumstances. God is never distracted by my the
things that cause me stress.

I like what Nelson Mandela observes. We can be
courageous even when we are in the grip of great fear.
All it takes, I believe, it to include that fear and act on
our convictions anyway. I believe Jesus was brave as he
walked to Golgotha. I believe Mary was brave when she
leaned over to look into the open tomb. I believe all of
us are brave when we hold fast to our faith and follow
the Prince of Peace anyway, despite criticism or
marginalization by those who disagree with us as we try
to follow the Christ.

**Let my fear reside in the midst of faith O God, and let
that embrace guide my steps forward.**

15.

3RD SUNDAY

"The Lord is risen indeed, and has appeared to Simon!" They
related the things that happened along the way, and how he
was recognized by them in the breaking of the bread.
— *Luke 24: 34-35*

❦

I believe in Christianity as I believe that the sun has risen: not
only because I see it, but because by it I see everything else.
– *C.S. Lewis*

My cousin Nora married a wonderful guy who was born
in Greece. Her faith journey has included sojourns in
many houses, including Buddhism (she is a doctor of
acupuncture) and the Greek Orthodox Church. In recent
years, she taught me the greeting her community uses at
Easter: "*Khristós anésti!*" Christ is Risen! To which one
responds, "*Alithós anésti!*" He is risen, indeed! You can
find this greeting in 57 languages on the internet.

I love the word "indeed!" I guess in Minnesota they
would say, "Christ has risen!" "Ya, ya, youbetcha!" My
Irish grandmothers would have said, "Christ is Risen!
Glory be to God!" Angel and Dick from Escape to the
Château would no doubt exclaim, "Christ has Risen!
Brilliant!"

What response will each of us craft this Easter season?
Perhaps this can be a mantra for the days ahead. "Christ
is Risen: Alleluia!" "Christ is risen! Just for me!" "Christ
is risen! Once and for all, in all times!" The creative
possibilities are endless.

*When the Easter season brings me glimmers of the
resurrection, in the earth greening and relationships
blooming, remind me to declare,* **"Khristós anésti!"**

16.

3RD MONDAY

Jesus answered them, "Most certainly I tell you, you seek me not because you saw signs but because you ate of the loaves and were filled. Don't work for the food which perishes but for the food which remains to eternal life." — *John 6:26-27*

❧

The nourishment of body is food, while the nourishment of the soul is feeding others. — *Ali ibn Abi Talib*

The homily at my niece Katie's first communion was incredibly memorable. The priest mentioned that his priest associate was sick, and that he was helping take care of him. He had purchased a lot of food for this purpose. Out of brown grocery bags came ice cream containers, cookies, what in my house we call "junky" cereal loaded with sugar, and a lot more. After pulling out about a dozen items, he asked the kids what they thought. They howled with laughter, and were quick to tell him that none of that food was a good choice; his friend needed healthy food. Perfect segue into the Eucharist as constant nourishment for our souls.

Perhaps I remember this homily that I heard decades ago because I am always in need of its simple message. Coming to Christ's table is an act of opening myself up to the power and healing he is always poised to offer me. It's a meal for the spirit, food for the journey. It is an act of solidarity and Christian family, as we all share the one bread and the one cup, together.

Feeding God, help me remember the power of your table, and bring me to it fully open to receive you.

17.

3RD TUESDAY

Jesus therefore said to them, "Most certainly, I tell you, it
wasn't Moses who gave you the bread out of heaven, but my
Father gives you the true bread out of heaven. For the bread
of God is that which comes down out of heaven and gives life
to the world." They said therefore to him,
"Lord, always give us this bread." — *John 6: 32-34*

❧

The sky is the daily bread of the eyes.
— *Ralph Waldo Emerson*

I've decided two things about God (among others): God
likes to feed and God likes to eat.

The evidence for the first is in both canons of
Scripture of course, whether it's the copious amounts of
manna and quail or the excessive loaves and fishes. Not
only does God like to feed humankind; nothing short of
an overflowing groaning board seems to do.

And God likes to eat. Someone once described Jesus
to me as "the itinerant Rabbi who eats his way across
Palestine." No meal is too simple; no company too
scandalous or too exalted for him. Pass the serving plate.

Eastertide reminds us to celebrate the gift of bread, as
we hear regularly from John's poetic, evocative "Bread
of Life" discourse. God's bread comes to us in infinite
ways, one of which is at a table on the Sabbath. Another
is the sky as Emerson mentions. The wide eyes of a
beloved pet. The musical laughter of a much-loved child.
The hand of an elder gently squeezed.

Lord, "give us today our daily bread…"

18.

3ʀᴅ WEDNESDAY

Jesus said to them, "I am the bread of life. Whoever comes to me will not be hungry, and whoever believes in me will never be thirsty. — *John 35*

❧

No one can know the infinite importance of a tiny drop of water better than a thirsty bird or a little ant or a man of the desert! — *Mehmet Murat Ildan*

I'm not often thirsty. I live in a world where clean water and an incredible array of beverages are in easy reach. But I remember a time when thirst had a whole new meaning for me. Pete and I were heading to New Mexico so I could meet his parents for the first time. We arrived at the Texas border, having traveled the length of that state at the hottest hour of that July day. No AC. No reprieve via opened windows in that very basic truck with its vinyl upholstery. As we pulled into a rest area, I was purple (well, practically) from the heat. I was beyond thirsty. I was wiped out. Pete grabbed the handle of the roadside water pump and began moving it up and down rigorously. "Stick your head under, honey, stick your head under!" he exhorted me. I realized I might be getting engaged to a madman. (He wasn't, I should add.)

Thinking about the magnitude of my thirst that day, I can't help but think how powerful Jesus' image of being living water for the thirsty might have been for his listeners. For people to whom every droplet mattered, how amazing an unending supply might have been. Suddenly his promise takes on expanded meaning.

Let me say with conviction this day, "My soul is thirsting for you, O God..."

19.

3RD THURSDAY

Therefore Jesus answered them, "Don't murmur among
yourselves. No one can come to me unless the Father who
sent me draws him; and I will raise him up in the last day.
— *John 6:43-44*

∽⤺

You were not born for murmuring, you are more than that.
— *Alan Maiccon*

My first associations with the word "murmuring" were
positive. Brooks murmured. Not sure what that meant,
but it sounded good! Then I read the Hebrew Scriptures.
I found a whole new meaning of murmuring. It's the
English translation of the Hebrew word *lun*, which
means the barely articulated complaints and mutterings
of upset people. It's the word used over and over to
describe the reaction of the Israelites that Moses is trying
to shepherd to the promised land. And it's the word
Mark uses to describe the fault-finding and discontent of
the Scribes and Pharisees.

I have to admit that in the past few years, my
murmuring has escalated to muttering and then to full-
blown loudly expressed mouthy malcontent. There are
more powerful ways for me to take action than t9hose. I
love Jesus' gentle admonition and I also love novelist
Alan Maiccon's observation, as well. We are not born for
murmuring. We are born for so very much more.

**When I am on the brink of murmuring (or more), draw
me close to you God and remind me that actions usually
are more effective than words.**

20.

3RD FRIDAY

"As the living Father sent me, and I live because of the Father, so he who feeds on me will also live because of me. This is the bread which came down out of heaven—not as our fathers ate the manna and died. He who eats this bread will live forever." *John 6:57-58*

❧

There are people in the world so hungry that God cannot appear to them except in the form of bread.
— *Mahatma Gandhi*

It seems like every culture has a bread. Flat bread, yeast bread. Nan, pumpernickel, soda, rye, challah, tortilla, pita. We could fill this book just with the names of bread.

There are many ways Jesus refers to himself in the cosmic language of the Gospel of John. One is "the bread of life." Given how central bread is to humanity, could any image be more powerful?

The bread that is the Christ fills our spiritual hunger. And that is beautiful. But the end goal is not only to have us feel satiated and satisfied. The "bread of life" is given to us so that we can turn outward to the world. First and foremost, we can feed those who are literally hungry. For the starving, there is nowhere else to start. And if those in need are physically sustained, we can feed them in countless other ways. We can turn to the weary, offering them sustenance and love. To the emotionally suffering we can offer compassion and care. The possibilities are unlimited.

This day, let me see and feed the hungry when I encounter them, O God.

21.

3ᴿᴰ SATURDAY

At this, many of his disciples went back and walked no more with him. Jesus said therefore to the twelve, "You don't also want to go away, do you?" Simon Peter answered him, "Lord, to whom would we go? You have the words of eternal life."
— *John 6: 66-69*

෨ඁ

He was leaving me. I wondered if I should stop him. If I should wrestle him to the ground and force him to love me. I wanted to hold his shoulders down and shout into his face.
— *Jonathan Safran Foer*

It seems, from the Gospel record, that literally thousands of people were drawn to Jesus. Some started walking alongside him at the beginning and were there to the very end. But I imagine others came and went. I think of the rich young man, who went away downcast. The folks who drove him out of town when they thought him too full of himself in the synagogue. Not everyone was able to go the distance.

It doesn't appear that Jesus chased, pursued, harangued or tried to persuade anyone to follow him. Want to follow? Great. Ready to walk off? Okay. No one is "wrestled to the ground" or forced to love him.

When Jesus asks Peter if the twelve are ready to take a hike. Peter is clear and firm. There is no where to go. No destination is better. No teacher more worthy of being with. This is a powerful witness for me, and a caution when I judge others.

When I face the urge to turn away from you and walk off, pull me close to you, O God: You have the words of eternal life.

22.

4TH SUNDAY

"I am the good shepherd. I know my own, and I'm known by
my own; even as the Father knows me, and I know the
Father. I lay down my life for the sheep." – *John 10: 14-15*

❧

You're not living until it doesn't matter a tinker's damn to you
whether you live or die. At that point you live. When you're
ready to lose your life, you live it. – *Anthony de Mello*

I have fallen out of moving cars twice in my life. The
second time, I had left the car in Drive and tried to climb
back in to put it in Park. The third attempt at climbing in
was the charm. The second, though, was a disaster as I
toppled out, landing hard on my shoulder, crushing it
and fracturing the bone. Yes, ouch. What I remember
most vividly is that entire episode was pure "lizard
brain." There was no thinking through what I was doing;
I was instantly in action. Bad action, as it turns out!

Once, I heard a spiritual leader admit that there was
only one person he could say, with certainty, that he
would die for. It was his wife. At the time, I had three
young children. Without a heartbeat's hesitation, I knew
I would die for them. Because I knew that before I
would weigh my actions, I would be in motion. Kind of
like the car episode.

Jesus exhorts us to lay down our lives more than once
in the Gospels. He's credible because he doesn't ask
what he himself isn't willing to do, revealing not only the
nature God but what it means to be a human being. That
includes countless forms of "losing our lives" for others.

Whether I live or die, God, let my life be for others.

23.

4ᵀᴴ MONDAY

"But one who enters in by the door is the shepherd of the sheep. The gatekeeper opens the gate for him, and the sheep listen to his voice. He calls his own sheep by name and leads them out." – *John 10: 2-3*

֍

There is nothing sweeter in this sad world than the sound of someone you love calling your name. – *Kate DiCamillo*

Did you have a childhood nickname? I had a few. Trish, of course. Later, Klodney and Clyde Crashcup the Great. Mean boys in the neighborhood called me Trash. My Grinch fan sister calls me Trishy Loo. My colleagues at Dow Jones called me Trish Bob. Trishter. A college buddy still calls me Trish the Dish. When I was in trouble with my father, I was Patreeeeeesha. To a certain wonderful sculptor I'm Babe. And, of course, I've been Mommy and now I'm Mom.

We know when our names are spoken in love. When Bobster left Trishter a message for her birthday, I was transported to my twenties and so many good times. When my eldest calls me Madre, I remember that little sweetie with the curly hair who ran into my arms – joyful and sad and everything in between – shouting Mommy.

I like to imagine God has some special, snazzy, and hopefully slightly sassy nickname for me. But God has some fun earthly competition in the aforementioned. Whatever that name, I trust that God never addresses me except to give me life and invite me closer.

God of many names, I pray to hear you when you speak my own.

24.

4ᵀᴴ TUESDAY

They came around him and said to him, "How long will you
hold us in suspense? If you are the Christ, tell us plainly."
Jesus answered them, "I told you, and you don't believe. The
works that I do in my Father's name, these testify about me."
– John 24-25

❦

And above all, watch with glittering eyes the whole world
around you because the greatest secrets are always hidden in
the most unlikely places. Those who don't believe in magic
will never find it. *– Roald Dahl*

There was a renowned magician in the 60s who referred
to himself as an "International Man of Mystery." (I
know, you thought it was Austin Powers.) I just love that
phrase. So sweeping and yet so vague!

I believe that while Jesus lived, there was an air of
mystery about him. There is a theme throughout the
Gospel of Mark that scholars refer to as the "Messianic
secret." No one seems to know who he is, and in fact he
discourages the disciples from making claims about him.
Mysterious. In John's Gospel, Jesus is the Word made
flesh; he was with and in God from the beginning of all
time. He knows who he is and he knows where he is
going. He chides those who can't seem to recognize him
as the Christ. What prevented them from seeing Jesus
clearly? Perhaps the sea of mental images they had of the
expected Messiah. Surely this rabbi with the rag-tag
followers didn't fit their pictures. He was a secret hidden
in plain sight; a Messiah in a most "unlikely" place.

**When I cannot seem to see you, O God, clarify my sight
and open my heart.**

25.

4ᵀᴴ WEDNESDAY

"I have come as a light into the world, that whoever believes in me may not remain in the darkness. If anyone listens to my sayings and doesn't believe, I don't judge him. For I came not to judge the world, but to save the world." – *John 12: 46-47*

✄

Make up a story... For our sake and yours forget your name in the street; tell us what the world has been to you in the dark places and in the light. Don't tell us what to believe, what to fear. Show us belief's wide skirt and the stitch that unravels fear's caul. – *Toni Morrison*

It strikes me that belief is sheer gift. From time immemorial, elders are called to pass on the faith of their ancestors. Deuteronomy tells us to fix God's word in our hearts and minds, and teach it to our children. Many of us have learned that we can share the faith, our faith, with our children or grandchildren, but we can't make them embrace it. That miraculous shift happens one heart, one soul, at a time, and it is God's work not ours.

Over the years I've met a lot of active, faithful Christians who are in pain over the way the generations that followed them have disconnected from the Church. It may seem scandalous, but I don't fret about this. I know I've done my best to share the sacred stories, the traditions and the beliefs that bring meaning to my life. I trust that the rest is in God's hands. How awesome to realize that even Jesus isn't overly hung up over what people believe.

God of justice and love, let my life witness to your presence and your power, and let me turn everything else over to you.

26.

4ᵀᴴ THURSDAY

"If I then, the Lord and the Teacher, have washed your feet, you also ought to wash one another's feet. For I have given you an example, that you should also do as I have done to you." – *John 13: 14-15*

❧

"So the small things came into their own: small acts of helping others, if one could; small ways of making one's own life better: acts of love, acts of tea, acts of laughter. Clever people might laugh at such simplicity, but, she asked herself, what was their own solution?" – *Alexander McCall Smith*

Scholars assert that the foot washing was the primary eucharistic ritual of the Johannine community, not the blessing and sharing of the cup and bread. Can you imagine what our self-concept would be if every time we gathered, we engaged in this ritual of humble service?

In our culture there is not a lot of opportunity for actual foot washing. So perhaps we have to expand our understanding to embrace this instruction more fully. Small acts of love of all kinds can be our response. A meal delivered to a family that is stretched to thin by illness or grief. Caring for the property of a neighbor who is aging and who is not as physically capable as they once were. Walking dogs. Caring for children. Tutoring. Helping a colleague meet a deadline. Taking a chore off the plate of our partner or child by doing it ourselves. Particularly the challenging or messy stuff.

When I want to limit myself to the more accessible, less messy task of handwashing, bring me dirty feet, my Lord.

27.

4ᵀᴴ FRIDAY

"Don't let your heart be troubled. Believe in God. Believe also in me. In my Father's house are many homes. If it weren't so, I would have told you. I am going to prepare a place for you. If I go and prepare a place for you, I will come again and will receive you to myself; that where I am, you may be there also. — *John 14: 1-3*

❧

Take one day at a time. Today, after all, is the tomorrow you worried about yesterday. — *Billy Graham*

Some of us are wired for worry. I certainly have been. I come from a long line of bona fide Irish worriers. After all, my people are the ones who went to sleep one night and woke up to find all their potatoes had turned black.

Enter the Serenity Prayer. What a healing balm that has been in my life! There are things I can change: I'll pray for the courage. There are things I can't change: I'll pray for acceptance. And the wisdom to know the difference? That's sort of a constant theme.

The second salve for worry in my life is meditation. When I rest in the silence, somehow I have more clarity and energy when I then confront the noise.

The third is "staying in the day." Doing what's there in front of me; what needs to be done now. The genius of "one day at a time" is that there is no other possibility for life; it only comes to us one day at a time!

Help me, God of many homes, to trust today and to surrender the things that cause me worry.

28.

4TH SATURDAY

Whatever you will ask in my name, I will do it, that the Father
may be glorified in the Son. If you will ask anything in my
name, I will do it. — *John 14: 13-14*

❧

Fate is like a strange, unpopular restaurant filled with odd little
waiters who bring you things you never asked for and don't
always like. — *Lemony Snicket*

"Ask for anything in my name, I will do it." The
danger of this verse is that it makes me want to relate to
Jesus like some sort of personal vending machine. That
can't be it!

The fourteenth chapter of John is the farewell
discourse of Jesus, who is inviting the disciples to align
everything they do with him and with God's will for
them. This saying has to do with the quality of their
prayer. Those who abide in God, and abide in his Christ,
are only praying for the will of God to be made manifest.
Sort of like we do in the Lord's prayer. We ask not for
our will, but that God's will be done through us.

Some days, I'd like to order up a winning lottery
ticket, an instant remedy for global warming, or a
wonder drug to instantly eliminate a pandemic. Life has
its bumps, big and small. Can I set aside my agenda, and
pray for the fullness of God's? Working on that.

**Let my prayer align with your hopes and dreams for me,
the people I love, and all of humanity, O God.**

29.

5TH SUNDAY

"Remain in me, and I in you. As the branch can't bear fruit by itself unless it remains in the vine, so neither can you, unless you remain in me. I am the vine. You are the branches."
– John 15: 4-5

❧

However strong the branch becomes, however far away it reaches round the home, out of sight of the vine, all its beauty and all its fruitfulness ever depend upon that one point of contact where it grows out of the vine. *– Andrew Murray*

My neighbor, who is a wine afficionado and also a can-do kinda guy, started growing grapes about a decade ago. No, we don't live in Napa, and yes, it gets pretty darn tundra like here in the winter, but he's had success. I think it's because he loves and babies those vines year round.

If Larry is capable of that sort of devotion to a plant, how much more so is God devoted to all of us. We just have to stay connected to the source. Yes, we might be at risk for deer nibbling and there are insect pests waiting to diminish our crop, but we can not only endure but flourish. We'll have years that yield abundantly and years where the fruits a bit sparse. We'll need some watering and feeding, and yes, there will be times that pruning is the best thing, but if we remain in Him, the harvest is promised.

I am yours, true vine: Keep me protected when the winds blow chill and nourish me in seasons of sunshine so that I might bear the fruit you hope from me.

30.

5ᵀᴴ MONDAY

"Have I been with you such a long time, and do you not know me, Philip? He who has seen me has seen the Father."
— John 14: 9

෨

To be loved but not known is comforting but superficial. To be known and not loved is our greatest fear. But to be fully known and truly loved is, well, a lot like being loved by God. It is what we need more than anything. It liberates us from pretense, humbles us out of our self-righteousness, and fortifies us for any difficulty life can throw at us.
— Timothy Keller

One of the things that is sort of amazing about having been with one partner more than three decades is that he knows me. I mean really. My joys. My pains. My passions. My moods. He knows my favorite dinner. He knows I hate to go to the grocery store. He knows that when things are scary or hard, I don't run, I get convicted.

He knows my strengths and my shadows. And it appears, by all measures, he still loves me.

Poor Phillip. I'm sure he didn't mean to irritate Jesus with his lack of recognition. I bet he even knew Jesus' favorite meals and personal quirks (he was human, after all, he had to have a few). But Phillip cannot seem to look beyond the surface to see the deep reality of Jesus' participation in the life of God.

Risen Christ, help me recognize the Divine in you, and help me recognize the divine life in myself and those around me.

31.

5TH TUESDAY

"Peace I leave with you. My peace I give to you; not as the
world gives, I give to you." – *John 14: 27*

∽

When we are at peace, we find the freedom to be most
fully who we are, even in the worst of times. We let go of
what is nonessential and embrace what is essential. We
empty ourselves so that God may more fully work within
us. And we become instruments in the hands of the Lord.
– *Joseph Cardinal Bernardin*

I have had glimpses of true peace. They have come to
me, for the most part, when I have found a way to
become still. Holding my youngest, an infant, after a
midnight feeding. Standing on the dock with the family,
gazing into the indigo sky of a up-north Minnesota night.
Sitting at the side of a woman who loved me with a vast,
mother's love as she flew into the arms of God.

Human beings seem to be wired for peace. The
scriptures describe the peace of God as a peace that
surpasses understanding. Something so vast and great
that it is beyond our limited comprehension.

That is the peace that Jesus gave us.

In the early church, the "passing of the peace" was a
loving kiss. Now it's a brief handshake or the waving of
fingers in the "V" peace sign to friends across the
sanctuary. Imagine if we really gave each other Christ's
peace. Arms thrown around each other, ecstatic love
poured out.

**On this Easter journey, make me an instrument of your
peace, O Lord.**

32.

5ᵀᴴ WEDNESDAY

If you remain in me, and my words remain in you, you will ask whatever you desire, and it will be done for you. — *John 15: 7*

❧

When Moses says, "Who am I that I should go to Pharaoh?"
God answers not by telling Moses who he is, but by telling
him who God is, saying, "I will be with you"
— *Rabbi Harold S Kushner*

The Greek word that is translated as "remain" in the Gospel of John means abide or dwell. In the culture we're in, it can be hard to make our home in Christ. The forces of Empire, strong in Jesus' day, pull on us just as insidiously, inviting us to compromise living our discipleship. I sometimes wonder if, just as in the first Century, it's gotten to be sort of uncool to be Christian. For me, that's due in part with the popular association of that word with fundamentalism and practices of exclusion. So when I introduce myself, I don't usually mention my faith. I don't know many people who do.

In the 12 Step community there is a principle that calls for "attraction not promotion." Let people see what we have, and they will want it and come to us. It grew a movement from two guys in Akron, Ohio nine decades ago to millions of people around the globe.

To dwell in God is to choose for hope, for peace, for joy. It's to do the hard thing when the hard thing is called for. It is to trust that God will provide the words and will always be with me. Even when it's uncool.

O God, as you helped Moses, help me to trust your presence and let your words dwell in me.

33.

5TH THURSDAY

"Even as the Father has loved me, I also have loved you.
Remain in my love. If you keep my commandments, you will
remain in my love, even as I have kept my Father's
commandments and remain in his love." — *John 15: 9-10*

❧

When your soul is resting, your emotions are okay, your mind
is okay, and your will is at peace with God, not resisting what
He's doing. — *Joyce Meyer*

Sometimes when I see people in the throes of new love,
I get a pang of jealousy. It's been a long time since love
occurred for me like an unfolding adventure.

I've come to appreciate what for lack of a better term
I'll call "old love." When my grandmother thought a
married couple were truly happy, she would say, "they're
like the old sock and shoe." I think my spouse and I are
getting closer to that. No, it's not a daily surprise of
getting to know someone. But this love that I've known
a long time is an amazing place to rest. I hope to remain
there for a long time to come.

I'm invited to remain in God's love with the same
appreciation and trust. To remain in God involves
following the path that Jesus has laid out for me. When
I'm living consonant with what He asks of me, I don't
fret about whether I'm doing His will.

I even occasionally get out of God's way.

**Easter me O God! Remain in me and help me live the
way you have shown me to live.**

34.

5TH FRIDAY

"Greater love has no one than this, that someone lay down his life for his friends." *– John 15: 13*

❧

This is the secret of life: the self lives only by dying, finds its identity (and its happiness) only by self-forgetfulness, self-giving, self-sacrifice, and agape love. *– Peter Kreeft*

For a long time, I read this text literally. After all, Jesus literally gave his life for those who were with him, for the Judean community and, in fact, for all of humanity.

It strikes me that the act of laying down one's life, the act of self-forgetting, of prioritizing others over ourselves, is a sort of "no half measures" proposition. It's sacrificial and selfless act. And not easy to do.

And yet we all have experience of self-forgetting. It's the rising of an exhausted parent who heads to a crib in the night when an infant awakes. It's letting go of our preference for something important so that another can have what they would prefer. Certainly it is anytime we forgive or show another mercy when we feel deeply wronged.

St. Francis goes so far as to assert that it is only in self forgetting that we "find."

Help me remember today, Resurrection God, that to lay down one's life is to die, in some way, so that another may live.

35.

5TH SATURDAY

"Remember the word that I said to you: 'A servant is not greater than his lord.' If they persecuted me, they will also persecute you. If they kept my word, they will also keep yours." – *John 15: 20*

∾

Do not get lost in a sea of despair. Be hopeful, be optimistic. Our struggle is not the struggle of a day, a week, a month, or a year, it is the struggle of a lifetime. Never, ever be afraid to make some noise and get in good trouble, necessary trouble. – *Rep. John Lewis*

Over the past two decades, I have gotten to know a lot of progressive Christians. Of all types. Catholics, for sure: Roman, Independent and otherwise. Lutherans of various sorts. Episcopalians and Methodists. Evangelicals breaking out of the box. Even Christian anarchists, a term I'm still trying to understand.

It's probably only the folks in that last group, if appearances are true, that don't really care if their Christian witness upsets people. I certainly care, probably too much (although I do my utmost to include that and speak anyway). Will what I have to say alienate someone? Will I be accused of being "too political" when in conversations about faith? At its founding, the Church was counter cultural. It was an active resistance to empire and critiqued the traditions from which it had emerged. It was not afraid to rock the boat. It was about what Rep. John Lewis called, "good trouble."

God keep me from despair and inspire me to "good trouble."

36.

6TH SUNDAY

"Even as the Father has loved me, I also have loved you.
Remain in my love." — *John 15:9*

❧

"I have decided to stick with love. Hate is too great a burden
to bear." — *Rev. Dr. Martin Luther King Jr.*

Recently, someone I respect and admire was slandered
on social media. I'm sure when people were writing their
dissing posts they didn't remember that screen shots
could send their comments not only all over the
platform they were using but off onto group texts. I was,
needless to say, righteously indignant.

My friend was a better Christian. He got on the phone
and communicated directly with the parties. And then he
let it go. I was still steamed, and he was moving on. Go
figure.

To remain in love is to build muscle in our ability to
release our grip. Even on justifiable anger, and to
certainly avoid, as Dr. King points out, the danger zone
of hate. Jesus laid out a few "woes" here and there, but
he also followed his path to the capital punishment
meted out by the Empire with acceptance and courage,
not hate. He asked us to pray for those who persecute
us, and he practiced what he preached, even o33n the
cross.

**God of forgiveness and acceptance, help me embrace the
path of love and nonviolence, wherever that path takes
me.**

37.

6ᵀᴴ MONDAY

"When the Counselor has come, whom I will send to you from the Father, the Spirit of truth, who proceeds from the Father, he will testify about me. You will also testify, because you have been with me from the beginning."– *John 15: 26-27*

✑

Stand before the people you fear and speak your mind – even if your voice shakes. – *Maggie Kuhn*

If Jesus was fully human, as we believe he was, then he experienced all the emotions of a human life. It is unimaginable to me that he would have stood before the Roman Governor and not been gripped by fear. And yet he spoke. He witnessed to the truth. Likewise, his followers went out into the Greco-Roman world speaking his transformative message to people who wanted to hear it, and to the distress of those for whom the status quo was threatened. Some of these witnesses died for preaching the Good News.

In our setting, none of us will die (hopefully!) for speaking the truth in love, particularly the truth of the Gospel. But our voices may shake as we tell people what we believe and why we believe it, and when we explain that our vision is a collective one – not a cozy opinion that applies only to us.

Our fear of speaking out will be overcome, I believe, if we remember who we are following and who is constantly at our shoulder, never separate from us.

If today I need to speak for you, God of transformation, hold me upright and strong even if my voice shakes.

38.

6TH TUESDAY

Nevertheless I tell you the truth: It is to your advantage that I go away; for if I don't go away, the Counselor won't come to you. But if I go, I will send him to you. — *John 14: 6-7*

❧

Only in the agony of parting do we look
into the depths of love. — *George Eliot*

I'm one of those "hate to say goodbye" people. Even in everyday circumstances. For years after Sunday Mass, I'd be lingering and chatting as the sanctuary emptied, kids eventually pulling on my clothes with a protracted "Mommmmm" to get me moving toward the car. I've also had quick goodbyes, such as having mercy on college Freshmen by not lingering too long.

And I've had sacred goodbyes. I've sat alongside people who were flying home into the divine life. One was a women I adored. I was at her bedside as her breath slowed. I looked at her peaceful face and remembered all the big and little things she had done for me and my family. Books — so many. Small china tchotchkes for my dresser. Lovely jewelry to commemorate special moments. Really good recipes for special occasions. A constant ear and wisdom gathered in experience. Dodie poured out love on me, and in the "agony of parting," I was present to the depth of it all. I was grateful.

I can imagine the pain of the community surrounding Jesus as they let go of him. But what a promise: That with the sending of the Spirit, they'd never truly be apart.

Today, help me remember that we can never be parted from you Easter Lord, and only temporarily from each other.

38

39.

6ᵀᴴ WEDNESDAY

"I still have many things to tell you, but you can't bear them now. However, when he, the Spirit of truth, has come, he will guide you into all truth…" – *John 16:12*

∽

Discovering the truth about ourselves is a lifetime's work, but it's worth the effort. – *Fred Rogers*

Just about every culture has as story designed to teach children to tell the "truth." In my upbringing, it was "The Boy Who Cried Wolf," one of Aesop's fables. We tell these stories to help them understand that the truth matters; that a world of other values sit on top of truth. Trust. Personal safety. The wellbeing of the group.

That story has a rather dire end. Wouldn't it have been great if the boy could have returned to the community, made amends, and learned from his lying ways?

The Spirit that Jesus sends is the Spirit of truth. That power is given to us not only to keep our commitment to Jesus fresh but to help us continue to grow in it. To be able to find the truth – about God, humanity, and more. Things will make sense in new and startling ways. We will find strength even if what we see challenges us about the world, about others, and as Fred Rogers so appropriately notes, ourselves.

Spirit of God, be with me and reveal your truth, particularly those things that will empower me to follow Christ more closely.

40.

6ᵀᴴ THURSDAY

"I tell you that you will weep and lament, but the world will rejoice. You will be sorrowful, but your sorrow will be turned into joy. A woman, when she gives birth, has sorrow because her time has come. But when she has delivered the child, she doesn't remember the anguish any more, for the joy that a human being is born into the world." – *John 16: 20-21*

❧

We cannot cure the world of sorrows,
but we can choose to live in joy. – *Joseph Campbell*

I've decided that it's not helpful to tell women in their first pregnancies birth stories. Everyone does it, as far as I can tell, but usually there's more agony described than joy. That said, my first two had craniums suited to their brains. I say no more. What I will say is that from the moment all three of my children were placed in my arms, everything about the preceding hours disappeared. All I was present to was the perfect gift of the amazing little people in front of me. Their wide eyes. The ways in which they looked like my people or his. I was fully in the "joy that a human being is being born into the world."

Now my job is to hold tight to that joy, that ecstasy that I've known. To trust that even when sorrow or hardship dominate my path, seasons of rejoicing return. To remember that every human person has been placed in someone's arms at one point or another. And to rejoice in that.

In these Easter days, O God, bring me moments of joy, and let me linger in the rejoicing.

41.

6TH FRIDAY

"I have spoken these things to you, that my joy may remain in you, and that your joy may be made full. This is my commandment, that you love one another, even as I have loved you." – *John 15: 11-13*

෨

People who love each other fully and truly are the happiest people in the world. They may have little, they may have nothing, but they are happy people. Everything depends on how we love one another. – *St. Teresa of Calcutta*

Both of my parents were children of immigrants. Neither family had a lot of stuff. My grandfather re-soled the kids shoes in the basement. A special hand-me-down toy or dress that arrived from my mother's aunts, who were baby nurses and secretaries for wealthy families, were shared not only among the siblings but the neighbors.

When friends have travelled on mission, something I would like to do but have not done outside this country, they've told me about the love and joy of the people with whom they lived despite impoverished circumstances. In our culture, too often we think joy will come from possessions. I have been hooked on "stuff" way longer than I care to admit. I've slowly learned that the joy of the love around me far exceeds the value of anything else. This lesson was driven home even more, for me, in the physical separation of the pandemic, which could not diminish the love.

On this day, let me reveal to another just how precious they are in my sight, and fully express my love.

42.

6ᵀᴴ SATURDAY

"In that day you will ask me no questions. Most certainly I tell
you, whatever you may ask of the Father in my name, he will
give it to you." – *John 16:23-24*

❧

Be patient toward all that is unsolved in your heart and try to
love the questions themselves, like locked rooms and like
books that are now written in a very foreign tongue. Do not
now seek the answers, which cannot be given you because you
would not be able to live them. – *Rainer Maria Rilke*

They must have been asking Jesus a lot of questions. I
know I would have. When I ask questions, I get clearer. I
also tend to retain information better. When I stay open
and inquire, I get to know people better. Issues resolve
easier. Children have no issue with asking questions. At
certain ages, they are a bubbling font of them. No
surprise his followers were constantly asking him things.

Some questions, of course, don't have easy answers.
They challenge us to the core. They pull us into places of
unknowing. They leave us stalled at a crossroads. I
believe God holds those questions with us, until all is
revealed.

I cherish Rilke's advice to a young friend. Most of our
experience with questions is that they are structures for
producing answers – anyone who has spent more than
five minutes in a classroom knows this! But to love the
questions... Perhaps that is what we do until the day
when, in Christ, there are no questions any longer.

**Inquiring God, help me sit in the peace of unknowing,
trusting that your path will be revealed to me.**

43.

7ᵀᴴ SUNDAY

So then the Lord, after he had spoken to them, was received
up into heaven and sat down at the right hand of God. They
went out and preached everywhere, the Lord working with
them and confirming the word by the signs that followed.
Amen. – *Mark 16: 19-20*

∽

God wants spiritual fruit, not religious nuts. – *Church Sign*

———————————

I am someone who would really, really like God to give
me a sign or two, just so I'm sure I'm on the right path.
Until recently, I was skeptical that signs from God exist.

Early in the life of our community, the Council
decided it would be nice to have an ambo. I spent
months on Craigslist looking for a wooden podium with
no luck. One week when I was particularly uncertain
about the my leap into ministry, I saw a lectern for sale.
It was in a town I associate with my mentor, about an
hour south. I wrote the seller and drove down.

When I got there, I almost fainted. It had been made by
the same craftsman from which my mentor and long-
time faith community had commissioned the sanctuary
furniture. When I asked where it was from, the seller said
"the church up the hill." It was the diocesan Cathedral.

I say it was a sign. From Tim, I believe. From Bishop
Ray, who also shaped my ministry. From their source,
where both dwell. I could almost hear them chuckling
over what an awesome sign they had generated!

**God of infinite love and humor, help me see your
affirmations when I most need them.**

44.

7ᵀᴴ MONDAY

Jesus answered them, "Do you now believe? Behold, the time is coming, yes, and has now come, that you will be scattered, everyone to his own place, and you will leave me alone. Yet I am not alone, because the Father is with me. – *John 16: 31-32*

∽

Let us be renewed by God's mercy… and let us become
agents of this mercy, channels through which God
can water the earth, protect all creation and make justice and
peace flourish. – Pope Francis

Do you think Jesus could have imagined the Church? Its vastness? Its outposts all over the globe? Its countless forms of cultural expression, music, artwork, language, complexion? Certainly, the reality we live in today was beyond the comprehension of the disciples.

The Christian community is, in many ways, at a juncture of rethinking itself and its mission. In recent decades, religion has become more voluntaristic. People are no longer driven by obligation or social pressure, or the belief that if they don't participate they will be condemned to eternal damnation.

I think that's good. I'm not sure any of those themes would have interested Jesus. What would though, is the idea that we come together as communities of love, justice and peace, working for the common good and to fulfill his vision for human kind. Working to become refreshing, open channels, as Pope Francis notes.

This day, "make me a channel of your peace," your justice, your mercy, O God.

45.

7ᵀᴴ TUESDAY

I glorified you on the earth. I have accomplished the work
which you have given me to do. Now, Father, glorify me with
your own self with the glory which I had with you before the
world existed. – *John 17 :4-5*

❧

A dairymaid can milk cows to the glory of God.
– Martin Luther

When you take a recording of crickets and slow it down
dramatically, the "chirp, chirp, chirp" transforms. It
suddenly sounds like a choir of singers, moving voices
that weave in, about, over, and under each other
gloriously. When I first heard this, I was awestruck. It
was evidence, to me, that all the creation is in fact made
to glorify God.

Humankind is considered by many to be the Divine
masterpiece. We may have the ultimate ability to glorify
God. One only has to bring to mind a Bach oratorio, a
Beethoven symphony or a Michelangelo sculpture

Or a well-baked soda bread. A beautifully hand-crafted
greeting card. A lovingly crocheted afghan. Hamburger
hotdish delivered to hungry friends. The hug of a
grandchild. The passionate theatrical performance of a
teen in the High School Musical.

Everything glorifies God. We just have to name it,
claim it, and offer it.

***Divine source of all human expression and creativity, let
my life glorify you today in things mundane and exalted,
offered to you with love.***

46.

7ᵀᴴ WEDNESDAY

"I am no more in the world, but these are in the world, and I am coming to you. Holy Father, keep them through your name which you have given me, that they may be one, even as we are." – *John 17: 11*

❧

You and I are all as much continuous with the physical universe as a wave is continuous with the ocean. – *Alan Watts*

Years ago, when on a retreat, I had a profound experience in meditation that left me convicted that separation is an illusion. Because we are, as my professor Fr. Kevin used to say, "body people," we tend to think individualistically. We are separate, one from another. We are separate from the environment, which we experience as sun, air, light, rain, etc. outside of ourselves.

But my experience left me with an overwhelming, gut-wrenching experience of unity, and a conviction that there is no separation in God's world. That includes the past and the future. It includes those who have gone before us and those who come behind us.

The cosmic joke is this: the idea that even if we tried, we could be separate – from the Christ, from the Christ in each other.

God who pulses in all things, let me experience oneness with you – in all things – this day.

47.

7TH THURSDAY

"Not for these only do I pray, but for those also who will believe in me through their word, that they may all be one. – *John 17:20-21*

❧

I found peace in praying for what my folks call "God's perfect will." As it evolved, my prayer has become, "Lord, let me live until I die." By that I mean I want to live, love, and serve fully until death comes. If that prayer is answered, if I am able to live until I die, how long really doesn't matter.
– Sr. Thea Bowman

What do you pray for? A number of years ago, it was suggested to me that I stick to the simple formula "thy will be done." But the truth is, I'm a little attached to my will being done. So I confess that I often call out to God with prayers that are far more detailed than "your will." Fortunately, I think God is very tolerant of me and my lists and longings. Even if occasionally God's response is "Thanks for sharing, kid."

I deeply admire Sr. Thea Bowman, whose life and ministry impacted so many, particularly African Americans and women. As she faced cancer, her prayer was to live until she died. How awesome. Imagine starting each day asking God to let us truly live, come what will. To get up, suit up, and "live, love, and serve fully." Interestingly enough, I suspect that is God's will!

God, let me seek your perfect will today, so that I might live, love and serve fully.

48.

7ᵀᴴ FRIDAY

Jesus said to Simon Peter, "Simon, son of Jonah, do you love me more than these?" He said to him, "Yes, Lord; you know that I have affection for you." He said to him, "Feed my lambs." – *John 21:15*

❧

I always have a funny story at communion time that underscores that no one is perfect, and that communion is not for perfect people but for hungry people. – *Greg Boyle*

Peter was a pivotal figure in the life of the early Church. He would, along with others, build a movement that would break out of Jerusalem and become a force throughout the Greco Roman world. And eventually the entire globe.

I take heart in Jesus' instructions to the man some will later call the first "Pope." No injunction to build soaring edifices or any other trapping of "kingdom." His simple request is that Peter "feed" his sheep; feed his lambs.

There is nothing more loving, perhaps, than feeding someone. Food is comfort, security, warmth. Food is the possibility of making it to another day. Of course we can be feed in more ways than by bread. We can be fed spiritually and psychically. And we can feed others, too, by providing nourishment in all these ways.

I wonder if Jesus focused us on feeding because it is, in fact, a joyful undertaking. To see people dig in, to see people lean back in satisfaction are beautiful things. That's soul food.

Today, let me lean in with generosity toward the hungry – whether that hunger is literal or spiritual.

49.

7ᵀᴴ SATURDAY

This is the disciple who testifies about these things, and wrote these things. We know that his witness is true. – *John 21:24*

∽

There's beauty everywhere. There are amazing things happening everywhere, you just have to be able to open your eyes and witness it. – *Sarah McLachlan*

I was once in a preaching class where a debate broke out about the scriptures and how we should read them. Some felt strongly about the historical/critical method; others wanted to related to them literally, reports of things exactly as they had happened. The professor said something unforgettable to the group: "All stories are true, and some of them really happened."

Her comment was freedom for me. From that point onward, I have related to the Gospel texts with new life. Their witness, to borrow the words of John, is true. In their pages are stories, accounts, parables, poetic discourses and more. All are there to illuminate my path, to make it easier to follow Jesus the Christ. And to witness to His transformative power.

All of these stories are true. And some of them really happened. However we chart the path to belief, what matters is that we find a way to embrace the power and mystery of what we've been given, and offer this truth to others.

When there is a moment for me to witness to You, to share Your beauty, let me share the truth I have experienced in your Word.

50.

PENTECOST SUNDAY

Jesus therefore said to them again, "Peace be to you. As the Father has sent me, even so I send you." When he had said this, he breathed on them, and said to them, "Receive the Holy Spirit!" – *John 20:21-22*

∾

Be who God meant you to be and you will set the world on fire. – *St. Catherine of Siena*

Fire is nothing short of amazing. Without it, humanity would no doubt have perished. It allowed us to stay warm. To cook food. To generate light. Circled around it, we built connections and community. We told our stories. We became who we are.

Fire is also a powerful force of destruction, as many regions of the world have experienced recently. It is difficult to contain and can consume everything in its path. It purifies, too. The refiners fire can leave unalloyed gold in its wake. Fire can kindle other fires.

There's a saying in our culture: People get burned out. But I've observed something. A burnt wick lights instantly. It doesn't take much time to reignite. I remain hopeful that when our faith feels flat or depleted, the same thing is true. In the upper room, people clustered in desperation and sadness. But in an instant, their zeal was reignited as the Holy Spirit came among them in wind and fire. As we come to the end of the Easter Season and embrace Ordinary Time, my prayer is that our faith, ignited by the resurrection and the journey to Pentecost, not only stays lit but burns brightly.

God of faith and fire, ignite your presence in me through your Holy Spirit today and always.

9 781736 905708